Personal Reflections of My Journey Through Breast Cancer

KEEPING
IT REAL

LAURA STARNER

Keeping it Real

Cover Design by Sprinkles On Top
Editing by Elizabeth Baker
Formatting by JT Formatting

ISBN: 978-1520509082

This book is a work of non-fiction. This publication is to provide
information about an experience through breast cancer by the
author. This book is not intended as a substitute for the medical
advice of physicians. The reader should regularly consult a
physician in matters relating to his/her health and particularly
with respect to any symptoms that may require diagnosis or
medical attention.

This book can be ordered by visiting my website:
http://laurasjourneyofhope.com

LAURA'S WORDS WILL INSPIRE AND ENCOURAGE OTHERS IN THE MIDST OF ONE OF LIFE'S CHALLENGES.

I met Laura nearly 20 years ago. I was beginning my second year of teaching and Laura joined our Kindergarten team after devoting time to be with her own children during their early years. Upon joining our staff, Laura made an immediate impact: for the students in her class, for our grade-level team and for me personally as my friend.

As a Kindergarten teacher, Laura was hard working, professional and always kept her kids and their families first. As a fellow team member, she was positive, collegial and helped us all grow and become better educators. As my friend, she was a mentor and trusted confidante. Although we only taught together for six years, those years were rich and full! We encouraged and supported one another through the arduous process of National Board Certification. We collaborated with one another to plan engaging lessons for our students and together we celebrated our students' progress! Not only did these six years afford me the opportunity to work alongside Laura professionally but I also had the opportunity to coach Laura's teenage daughter who was a member of our local varsity high school team. Seeing Laura outside of school, in the role of parent, only deepened my respect. Now with two young children myself, I strive to instill the same values that Laura instilled in her girls. Paige and Kelsey are now two accomplished, independent, confident and compassionate young women with careers and beautiful families of their own.

Although our professional careers eventually took different paths, we remained close. I always knew that Laura was destined for leadership positions that would enable her to touch the lives of even more children and impact the professional lives of more educators. Laura set this path in motion when she left her teaching position and became a reading coach, sharing her literacy expertise with her K-5 colleagues. It was during this time that she also completed her degree in Educational Leadership. She then became an Assistant Principal at a highly successful elementary school before eventually leading her own school as principal. Laura's success was a direct result of her passion for education, her work ethic, her tenacity and her focus on all things positive.

These same characteristics, as well as her unshakeable faith and the support of her family, carried her through her breast cancer diagnosis, treatment and now her outreach as a SURVIVOR!

Laura's journey is a remarkable one. I am so thrilled that she has chosen to draw upon her collective experiences as a wife, mom, educator, cancer survivor and woman of faith to share her story of hope as a way to support, educate and inspire others. She certainly has touched my life in this way and for that, I am grateful. Thank you, Laura. I am honored to call you my friend.

Dr. Katy Cortelyou, Education Consultant

What a blessing it was that Laura Starner's career and life should intersect with mine. As a lifelong educator, I have had many professional and personal relationships. Sometime during the 1999 school year a fellow principal and I had an important conversation about the amazing teachers that we were privileged to work with at our respective school settings. We were extolling the talents and abilities of a young group of professionals who were some of the finest educators we had ever come across. Listing their skills and gifts ran the gamut from literacy specialists, classroom managers, optimists, communicators, compassionate thinkers, problem solvers, to creators of real world scenarios, and the list goes on. My friend mentioned that several of her superstars were making the move from classroom assignments to resources specialists and on to assistant principals. She shared several names with me.

Fast-forward five years and I was fortunate to be able to select one of these superstars as my assistant principal: Laura L. Starner. Laura's professional journey was amazing: a classroom teacher with the magic touch, the consummate reading coach and resource for struggling students; organized, supportive curriculum specialist at a newly created elementary school; firm, loving, and positive shaper of young character in an ethnically diverse school setting; engaging facilitator for professional development; and conciliator among and between teachers, students, parents, and community.

Oh, did I mention that during this time she also raised two successful, compassionate daughters, supported a husband on the corporate fast track, raised up her friends and loved ones whenever needed, she trusted God and lived her faith, and … yes, she also fought a long, brave, horrific fight against stage three breast cancer. She faced every challenge, every adversity, every setback with hope and praise for her Lord and Savior.

In the midst of her hard fought battle, her faith was tested, but she came out the other side with a refined sense of her role in God's world. It was during this fight that Laura also assumed the leadership role of principal of one of the largest elementary schools in her district. She began to write and share her joys and sorrows while always standing on the Word. We can all learn and benefit from the experiences of this woman of faith; teacher of all children; leader in public education; a loving mother, wife, and now Grandma!

Debra Edmiston
Senior Director of Elementary Education, Retired

Laura Starner's story about her journey through breast cancer struck me on all emotional levels. Not only is she an accurate and prolific note keeper, but she also put her experience into words so that I was able to understand even the technical terms. In the process, I learned to understand my own body a little more.

When I picked up the book and started reading, I could not put it down. I had to know what happened next and sometimes I just let tears roll down my cheeks.

While I was Laura's supervisor in the school system, she never complained and was just as accurate with her school record keeping. She was at work and it was unknown that she critically made her appointments for after school hours so that the effects of treatment mainly happened on weekends. She is the ultimate professional.

This story is a must read not only for someone who is diagnosed with cancer, but for every woman and man. It could change your life as it has mine!

Diana Hill Myrick
Retired, Senior Director
Polk County Elementary Schools

My colleague, co-leader at our school, and friend, Laura, didn't know how easy or hard the path would be after her cancer diagnosis, and there were days it was really hard. But through it all, she remained committed as possible to the responsibilities of her job as Assistant Principal, and she kept me focused (as she always did) on remembering the students and the importance of their learning, even when the challenges of running a large school seemed to take center stage.

Her knowledge and love of children's learning has always made her heart beat, and she carried her passion and strength into her next professional opportunity as a Principal at a neighboring school after her treatment and recovery. I'm grateful for the intersection of our lives and am confident her words will inspire and encourage others in the midst of one of life's challenges.

Julie Ward

DEDICATION

I walk for all who are **fighting** breast cancer.
I walk to celebrate all **survivors** and to remember those
who **lost their battle** to this horrible disease.

This book is dedicated to...

My loving husband,
who stayed by my side through this horrible disease and
remains by my side to this day.

My children,
who provide a constant source of joy and pride.

My mom, my rock,
who taught me to be a strong woman of faith.

My mother--in-law,
who always treats me like her own daughter.

My friend, Moe,
who was a source of encouragement and
a good listener.

And...

In memory of my dad,
who was gone too soon and never knew that I would be a
6+ year survivor.

ACKNOWLEDGMENTS

Thank you to the following individuals,
without whose support and contributions this book would
never have been written:

Mrs. Melissa Capps
Dr. Katy Cortelyou
Mrs. Debra Edmiston
Mrs. Diana Myrick
Dr. Sherrie Nickell
Mrs. Michelle Townley
Mrs. Katherine Riley
Mrs. Julie Ward

TABLE OF CONTENTS

INTRODUCTION

Family Picture, 2008
Kelsey (L), Paige (R), Doug and me
This photo was taken one month before my breast cancer diagnosis.

I was 47 years old when I was diagnosed with In-
vasive Ductal Carcinoma. This type of breast
cancer is best described as breaking through the
wall of the milk duct and invading the tissue. Breast
cancer did not run in my family and I nursed both of
my daughters. I did not think this would ever happen
to me.

By the time I was diagnosed, the cancer was
Stage 3a and Grade III. Stage 3a (advanced stage) is
referred to as locally advanced breast cancer. Grade

III breast cancer is a very aggressive form of cancer. The silver lining in all of this is that it was triple positive cancer, fast growing with positive estrogen receptors.

Even the first doctor I saw told me how **LUCKY** I was that it was breast cancer because I could probably survive at least five years.

Well, in these last five years, I have been blessed to be able to plan and attend the weddings of both of my daughters, witness the graduation of my youngest daughter from The University of Florida and have become a doting grandmother to our three grandchildren. So, when I add **#Blessed** to a post or picture, it means that I am thankful for every minute.

I recently celebrated being a six-year cancer survivor. I hope my story will serve as a blessing, an inspiration, and most importantly, an encouragement to you.

WHY I SHARE MY STORY NOW

Six-Year Breast Cancer Survivor

When you receive a diagnosis of cancer, your life **changes forever**. From that point on, you are no longer known as a wife, a mother, a daughter, an educator, or a friend—you simply become "the one who has cancer." Some people deal with it by talking to everyone about every detail. That just wasn't me.

I remember sitting in my office, the Assistant Principal's office, telling the principal and the secretary that my chemo, in all reality, would take 15 months. A school is like a small city, a community, and a family, all rolled into one. We spend as much time with each other as a staff as we do with our own families. We are close to one another and care about each other. As I told them that for the next year or more, I would have to go to the cancer center and receive various forms of chemo through my port, I fell apart. I just sat there and sobbed. I knew my health was more important than my job, but I loved my job. I loved working with teachers and seeing the students every day.

My way of updating the staff and friends at other schools was to designate my precious friend Gale to send updates in order to keep everyone informed of my progress. My dear friend Moe shared updates with a few of the fellow assistant principals in our school district, as well. I prayed, spoke as if I was already healed and immersed myself in worship. I am a woman of faith and I put my trust in God to bring about His divine will.

It has taken years for me to be able to talk about my diagnosis and progress without tearing up. I eventually became the principal at my own school. I began to share my story with those who needed words of encouragement. I discovered that **inner healing** began to take place every time I reached out to help others. Now, I can passionately tell my story and, in doing so, I have become stronger. Upon reflection, maybe some of my hesitancy was because I was only given a 56% chance to live five years.

Now, I am ready to share my story and help others. While the journey is different for each individual, personal boundaries should always be respected. I am finding comfort in telling my story now; and, I believe this comfort comes from one of my favorite verses.

1 Timothy 4:16 (Living Bible)
"Keep a close watch on all you do and think.
Stay true to what is right and
God will use you to help others."

FOREVER CHANGED

Lifesaving Loofah…Now Retired

It was a normal morning in November of 2008. While I was in the shower getting ready for the day, I reached for my loofah and shower gel. No loofah! It was across the bathroom in the tub and I was in such a hurry. I just put some shower gel in my hand. As I moved my hand under my right arm, I felt a lump. I thought to myself… **that's odd**. Then I compared it to the left side and something was definitely different with my right side. I quickly got dressed and went to work. I was the only administrator at school that day so I had no other option. By the time I was able to contact my primary care doctor, I made an appointment for December 3rd. My primary care doctor sent me for a CAT scan, suspecting that it was lymphoma, and a mammogram. I had just had a mammogram in March and I was very vigilant to get one every year.

During the mammogram on December 17th, a lump was detected in my right breast and two suspicious masses were found in my right axilla. The radiologist wanted to do biopsies that day, but I was in shock. Even now, I can still picture myself crouched in the corner of that room, as the radiologist insisted I get the biopsy done right then. I scheduled a biopsy for December 19th before I left. In the meantime, I got ready for Christmas and for Paige's (our eldest daughter) graduation from nursing school. I only told my husband and my dear friend, Moe. They were to become the foundation of an amazing support team.

Paige and I at her graduation from nursing school

Biopsy Results

On December 26th, while in my car doing some after Christmas shopping, I received a call from my doctor's nurse. She asked if I had been contacted regarding my biopsy results. I told her that no one had called yet. She said that my doctor was out of town but she would have the doctor on call contact me later in the day. The call came that afternoon while I was at home with Kelsey, our youngest daughter. He was very apologetic for delivering the news over the phone as he went on to tell me that I had breast **cancer**! Of course I was full of questions... How bad is it? What stage is it? What now? He admitted that he didn't know how to read the pathology report but that he didn't want me to worry. *Really? Didn't want **ME** to worry?* He so doesn't know me. I'm a little on the **Type A**, obsessive side. He went on to say that many of his patients were breast cancer survivors of 10, 20 and even 30 years. An appointment was scheduled with a Surgical Oncologist for Monday. It was Friday and I would have to wait until Monday to find out details. All I could think about was how I would tell my husband, my children, my mother, and other family members and friends.

After I hung up the phone, tears streamed down my face. I sat in the front room and stared out the window and I prayed! I remembered a song that we used to sing in church when I was a little girl.

"Peace, peace, wonderful peace coming down from the Father above. Sweep over my spirit forever I pray in fathomless billows of love."

You see…I am a believer…a Christian…a person of strong faith and I prayed….

Telling Others of My Diagnosis

When my husband, Doug, came home from work, I told him that I indeed had breast cancer. I do not remember his full reaction but I know he told me that everything would be all right. We told the girls that night and I can completely recall their reaction. Kelsey (17 at the time) just sat there and looked at me and Paige (who was 21) said, "So, you are going to die?" I replied, "I don't **plan** to die. God **will** heal me." The next night Doug and I went to tell my mom. I didn't want to give her that news over the phone. Doug's side of the family was in New Mexico so I had to tell them by phone.

It was a long weekend.

THE DIAGNOSIS

On Monday, December 29, 2008, I went to see the Surgical Oncologist. As I sat in the waiting room, I saw despair on the faces of so many people. While I was waiting for my name to be called, I prayed for everyone in the room. I prayed silent prayers that God would intervene in each of their situations. In 1 Thessalonians 5:17, the Bible tells us that we should "pray continually" according to the New International Version. I would learn the true meaning and impact of this scripture, as I was about to face the biggest challenge of my life.

Surgical Oncologist

"Laura Starner?"

I heard the nurse call my name. I gathered my belongings and walked back to the exam room. Doug and my mom followed me. The doctor was very cold and factual. He opened the conversation with, "So, you are aware that you have breast cancer?" Doug and my mom stepped out of the office so he could examine me. After the examination, they came back in the room. He said, "Well at least it's breast cancer. You are **lucky** that it is *just* breast cancer because most patients live at least five years. It is the best cancer to have."

Did I just hear him correctly? There is a **best cancer** to have? Really? I'm sure he meant... most curable or from a medical stand point, most advanced in diagnosing. Surely, he can't think it's good to have cancer?!

He went on to give us some facts about my case in particular:

• There were three tumors... one in the right breast about half the size of a AA battery, two in the right axilla, one was about the size of a 9 volt battery and the second was about half the size of a AA battery

• It was Stage III, which is very aggressive because as it wasn't there on my last mammogram, which was in March, then it is fast moving

• Since it was already in the lymph nodes, I needed a Bone Scan and PET Scan or Positron Emission Tomography, to make sure it hadn't spread to the bone, liver or lungs

I just sat there **numb**, wishing my mom did not have to hear all of this information. I wanted to protect her from the bad news. I knew Doug would be positive and draw on his faith, but nobody wants to hear this about his or her own child.

The oncologist asked me which chemo doctor I wanted to see. He went on to explain that there were two very renowned, traditional male doctors and one female doctor. I asked him if the female doctor had a daughter. He said, "I don't know, I will check for you." When he came back in he said, "Yes, she has a daughter and she will see you Wednesday because we need to get things started." He said, "I'm just curious. Why did you ask if she had a daughter?" I replied, *"Because I want her to treat me as she would treat her daughter if she was sick."* To that he replied, "I never thought of it that way."

Before we left his office, I had an appointment with the Oncologist-Hematologist to establish my treatment plan and with the general surgeon for port insertion surgery. That would be my last visit with him because I changed to a surgeon who specialized only in breast cancer. When we got outside, we all went our separate ways. Mom went to the church, Doug went to Publix to get food and I drove home all by myself with a feeling of utter disbelief.

In retrospect, on December 29th, I became my own advocate and started researching doctors and surgery options.

LIFESAVING DECISIONS

On December 31st, I was scheduled to meet with the Hematologist-Oncologist. She worked me in as her last appointment on New Year's Eve day. I did my research on her because I felt that choosing the right chemo doctor could be a **lifesaving** decision—and it was. I learned that she completed her fellowship at NYU and there were no sanctions or malpractice claims in the last 14 years. She sounded perfect on paper. Of course, the real test would be when we met face to face.

As I sat there with Doug and my mom, I was prepared for the waiting room this time. Once again it was full of people who looked anxious and there was a sense of desperation in the air. After my last experience at the Oncologist, I had gone home and loaded Praise and Worship music on my MP3 player so I could zone out with my earplugs and music while I waited. I again prayed silent prayers for everyone in the waiting room, something I did every time I went to the Cancer Center. My mom wanted to talk but I just wasn't in a state of mind for small talk and to be totally honest, I was too scared to speak.

"Laura Starner?"

When I heard the nurse call my name, I got up and left Doug and my mom in the waiting room. I had written down questions ahead of time and I promised Doug that I would take good notes. When the doctor entered the room, she greeted me with a smile and a firm handshake. She reviewed my chart and examined me. She asked me how I had found the lump under my arm (right axilla). I told her the story of the loofah, how I had left it across the bathroom so I had just put gel on my hand. She said, "Good job."

Then she went into a lot of medical jargon, explaining the need to get that port in right away because we need to start chemo ASAP. Chemotherapy before surgery would kill any cancer cells that may have spread beyond the lymph nodes even if they were not detected by imaging or laboratory tests. So, it could increase the chance of long-term survival by preventing a recurrence. She went on to outline my treatment plan:

Adriamycin/Cyclophosphamide (AC) – four cycles …one dose every two weeks to last a period of two months

Taxol and **Herceptin** – four cycles…one dose every two weeks to last a period of two months

Herceptin – to continue for one year
Surgery – to be discussed after we see the effects of the chemo

Radiation – 35 rounds… after surgery –YES, you read that correctly… 35 rounds which means 35 days in a row, taking Saturday and Sunday off (woo hoo!) **In addition to the treatments, she also ordered more tests:**

In addition to the PET scan already ordered, I would need a MUGA scan, Multi-Gated Acquisition Scan, which is a test to check how well the heart chamber (left ventricle) pumps blood through your body at rest. It also determines the size and shape of your heart. You see the AC chemo, commonly referred to as **Red Devil**, is very strenuous on the heart. I would also need an echocardiogram every 3 months to monitor my heart health.

The doctor was positive and confident that we were going to take care of this.

After hearing about the treatments and various tests, there was one very important question on my mind: I asked, "Can I continue to work through chemo?" She said that she had many patients who work through chemo and absolutely encouraged me to continue working. It was my decision.

As I left the exam room and joined Doug and my mom in the waiting room, I was smiling. This was the exact opposite of the way I felt just two days ago.

They looked puzzled. I said, "She's wonderful and kind and we have a plan. Everything is going to be okay." I was relieved and confident that God led me to the best doctor.

MAKING SENSE OF IT ALL

Chemo Education

Before you start chemo, you have to attend Chemo Education. I had never heard of Chemo Education before this experience. Chemo Education is scheduled with a nurse and my nurse was the sweet nurse from Dr. Wonderful's office. **(I affectionately referred to her as "Dr. Wonderful.")** Doug went with me to Chemo Education because the clinic suggests that you bring at least one of your caregivers with you. I had my calendar with notepaper in the back and I was ready to take notes.

The nurse explained that I would need:

• Four weeks of AC chemo every other week. This chemo may cause you to experience the following side effects: sores in your mouth, loss of nails, nausea, vomiting, fatigue, body aches and pain… and you will lose your hair. This chemo is known as **Red Devil**. After each cycle of this chemo, I would need Neupogen shots. (Neupogen shots stimulate the production of white blood cells. The shots would be needed for five and seven days after each treatment, depending on the results from the lab work.)

• Four cycles of Taxol and Herceptin (No extra shots with this chemo. YAY!) This chemo has similar side effects as the AC chemo. I learned that my hair would not begin to grow back until this chemo was out of my system.

Please Note: Everyone responds differently to chemo. The nurse did say to eat protein and foods that contain potassium. Also, she directed that my acrylic nails must come off immediately. I loved my nails. They were among my favorite and most essential accessories!

Information Overload and How to Organize it All

As I returned home with handfuls of information, I realized that I should organize all of this information so I could find it as needed. I had a couple of small piles already.... chemo info, notes from two doctors and my mammogram and CT (Computerized Tomography Scan) report. I decided to organize the information in a three-ring binder.

I set up the notebook according to the following categories:

1. Meds

2. Doctor visits – I took notes at every conversation with each doctor, filed it by date in the notebook and put a copy of the notes and the lab reports in a plastic sleeve.

3. Copies of all Tests…CT Scans, PET Scans, MUGA Scan, Pathology Reports, Echocardiogram, etc.

4. Miscellaneous Information

I took my notebook and calendar to every visit. I had questions written ahead of time so that I didn't forget anything. As I sat in the chemo chair receiving the infusion of chemo, I organized my notebook. When I got my very first chemo, my nurse, Jerry, asked me what my notebook was for and I told him that I take notes at every doctor visit and ask for a copy of my chemo orders and all lab results. His response was along the lines of, "That's a good idea because we aren't Jesus Christ. We aren't perfect."

In the front of the notebook, I had a three-ring pencil pouch so that I would always have my writing tools and a three-ring business card holder. I kept a business card from every doctor and everyone affiliated with my treatment. If I needed to clarify something or there was an emergency, I would know whom to call.

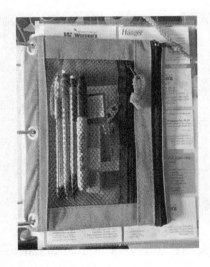

You are in Charge of Your Health

The most important thing that I want you to remember is that YOU are in charge of your health care decisions. Do your homework. Educate yourself on your specific condition. Research your doctors. Be an advocate for yourself or designate an advocate if you feel overwhelmed. <u>You</u> are more than a statistic. <u>You</u> are so important to God that even the hairs on your head are all numbered.

> *"And even the very hairs of your head*
> *are all numbered"*
> Matthew 10:30 NIV

THE NEW NORMAL

Meeting Red Devil Chemo

By January 12, 2009, the **port** was in place and we were ready to go. A *port-a-cath* is a small medical appliance inserted near the left clavicle with a tube that goes directly to the **superior vena cava,** a large vein carrying deoxygenated blood from the head, arms and upper body into the heart. This positioning allows the infused chemotherapy to be spread throughout the body quickly and efficiently and that's what I needed.

My Chemo Routine

Thursday, January 15th was my first chemo treatment. I went to school that morning and stayed the majority of the day because I had made a late afternoon appointment. I left work early enough to go home, take a shower, get alone with God and listen to my Praise and Worship music. In fact, this would become my routine before each chemo. Each time I would pray, "Now God, if this is all a mistake and when I get there they are so apologetic, I won't even be mad…but, if I do need to go through this experience, I trust you and rely on you to give me strength." I am after all, only human. Yes, I'm a Christian and I need to practice what I preach but I am human, therefore, I rely on God for strength. Before I knew it, my mom was at my house to pick me up and we were on our way.

When I arrived at the doctors' office, the nurse brought out a pill for me to take (Emend) so I would have it in my system before my treatment. This would help with the side effects of nausea and vomiting.

It was my turn to see the doctor. I went back to the office and Dr. Wonderful asked me how I was doing. I confessed that I had heard so many negative stories about chemo and I was scared. She reassured me that everything was going to be all right. She reviewed my lab work to make sure my blood counts could sustain the first dose of **A/C (Red Devil)** chemo. She ordered more testing: Bone Scan, Breast MRI and BRCA testing (a gene test to check for specific changes or mutations in genes that help control normal cell growth). After all, I had two daughters at home and we needed to know if I carried the BRCA gene. She also gave me a prescription for an anti-nausea pill to take for 24-48 hours after chemo.

Dr. Wonderful reminded me that I should have minimal contact with the public because of the risk of infection. This meant **NO** to the following:
• Trips to the grocery store

- Eating out

- Drive thru

- Church (well, I still went to church for a while but I avoided all of the handshaking/greetings)

Chemo Lab

The chemo lab was ready for me. My mom and I walked to my designated chair and were greeted by Jerry, one of the best chemo nurses. As he was attempting to access my port, he said, "I'm going to need a long needle." I know that I went pale and I looked at my mom with fear in my eyes. She excused herself to go get some water or a snack, anything other than seeing her daughter start the dreaded chemotherapy.

By the time she got back, I was all hooked up to **Red Devil chemo.** It was literally **RED**. Jerry brought me a warm blanket. I inserted my ear buds, reclined my chair, and zoned out to my Praise and Worship music. I also updated my notes, lab reports and chemo orders from my doctor's visit in my notebook. Jerry checked on me frequently since this was my first time to receive A/C chemo. When I was almost done with my treatment, he told me to go eat a non-greasy, good healthy meal with lots of protein. He reminded me that it might be all I have to eat for a few days. I took his advice and had a very healthy meal.

When I got home, I visited with my girls and my husband. Around 10:30 PM, an indescribable feeling came over my body. It was like the room was spinning and I felt like a 50 pound blanket was covering me. Per Jerry's advice, I went straight to bed. I didn't want to vomit/get sick so I stayed very still. My mom came in with the anti-nausea medicine and I really didn't want to move to take it because I didn't want to get sick. Every time I moved my head, I felt an overwhelming feeling of nausea that I could barely hold back. So, I remained very still!

The next morning, my mom came to stay with me and brought me some pears to eat with the anti-nausea medication. Grape Gatorade was the only thing that felt good on my stomach. When I would eat or drink, I would try not to lift my head any more than necessary. When someone would come in the room to talk to me, I would not move my head to look at them. They would have to move to my direct line of vision.

I slept the next day (Friday) until about 1:00 PM. I sat out in the living room for a couple of hours and tried to eat something and soon headed back to bed. Saturday, I spent most of my time sitting up in my special chair in the living room. I still had a strong feeling of nausea. On Sunday, I went to church, avoiding all of the hand shaking. Later that afternoon, my dear friends Debbie and Moe brought an amazing meal of baked turkey, mashed potatoes and rolls. I was feeling good enough to eat a little more each day.

I returned to work on Monday trying to keep life as normal as possible. And so the new normal began. The Neupogen shots arrived at my house and Paige started the injections Monday night. I am so blessed that she graduated from Nursing School on December 11, 2008. God knew that she would be essential to my recovery. God is so good!

Pink became my signature color and grape Gatorade became my best friend.

Daughters: Nurse Paige and Kelsey...love these girls

Friends Making a Difference

After the side effects of the January 15th chemo subsided, the next two weeks were pretty normal. I was working every day and the school secretary made pink curtains for my office. She was so thoughtful. I was learning to embrace the *pink*. During chemo education, I was given suggestions for some wig shops in town. My friends Debbie and Moe, met me at the wig shop after work so that I could order my wigs and have them ready when my hair fell out. With **A/C Red Devil** chemo, I could expect my hair to fall out between two and three weeks and I wanted to be prepared. I had already ordered turbans to wear at home so I could be comfortable.

Prayer

My church always participated in a two week fast in January. The fast was coming to a close with a special service on January 25, 2009. The service was a time of worship and prayer. I was 10 days out from my first treatment so Doug, Kelsey, and I went to church that night. At the end of the service, Pastor asked for those who needed prayer to come forward. There were so many people who went forward and I was one of them. I'm not sure how it happened but I ended up right in front of my Pastor. I told him that it was aggressive breast cancer and he began to pray. When he was finished, I turned around to see that Kelsey was crying. **I hugged her** and told her that **I was going to be fine**. Two of our dearest friends came down to support us. They had not yet heard of my diagnosis. We briefly updated them and returned to our seats.

As I went to bed that night, I asked God to renew my blood with his healing power as it flowed through my body while I slept. I thanked him for healing me and giving me strength to get ready for my next treatment on Thursday. About 2 AM, I woke up to the extraordinary feeling of **warmth circulating** through my body. It started in my right leg and went all through my right side and through my mid-section. It was like the blood was flowing through my circulatory system. I just cried and thanked God for his healing power. I will **never forget** that night and I have never shared it with anyone before. It was a defining moment in my journey that assured me that God had my back and I would be okay.

Second Chemo

Before I knew it and ready or not, it was Thursday, January 29th…time for my second chemo. It was the same routine on January 29th as it was on the 15th:

- I worked most of the day.

- I left work in time to take a shower and to listen to my Praise and Worship music.

- My mom came and picked me up because I couldn't drive myself.

- I met with Dr. Wonderful to review my blood work.

• I went to my assigned chair in the chemo lab and got started with the A/C (Red Devil) chemo infusion.

• Then, I went home to eat dinner, provided by the dear staff at my school. They sent food home with me every Thursday.

This treatment hit me sooner than the last one. I went to bed about 8:30 PM and stayed there. I only moved to take the anti-nausea medicine and sip my grape Gatorade. I lay very still so as not to get sick. This treatment hit me with extreme nausea and fatigue. I stayed in bed, only eating when I had to take meds, and didn't get up until noon the next day, Friday. Saturday, I sat in my special chair in the living room and rested. There was no need to try to be a hero.

Not-So-Boldly Bald

My wig order was due Saturday and I was to pick them up on Sunday. I wanted to bond with my girls in a hair cutting celebration but it didn't really turn out to be a celebration. It was still **too raw** for all of us. The girls didn't really want to cut my hair so Kelsey took the pictures and Paige reluctantly began to cut my hair. All of us had to hold back tears and we tried to smile through the tears.

I admire all of the women who journey through this disease and boldly go bald. That just wasn't me. After my head was completely shaved, I joined Doug and his mom in the family room. I was wearing a soft beige turban. Turbans and wigs were part of the **new normal**.

COMPLICATIONS AND JOY ALONG THE WAY

Complications with my PORT

I noticed that my port incision was not healing so I scheduled an appointment with Dr. Wonderful. I didn't want anything to stand in the way of my treatments **staying on schedule**. I went to see her on February 10, 2009 and she was very concerned because the incision was still open and had suspicious drainage. She wanted me to go back to the surgeon who put the port in, but I was NOT going back to that doctor! So I called to get a second opinion from a well renowned breast surgeon. She was willing to work me into her schedule the next day. Yes, she was also a female doctor. This was a great visit with the doctor who would eventually perform my surgery. She felt that the port drainage was healing normally and did not seem concerned. She went on to discuss my diagnosis and surgical options. We would revisit all surgical options after the BRCA testing results were back and after chemo.

The next day was my regularly scheduled appointment with Dr. Wonderful and for my chemo treatment. I went through the usual routine:

- Worked most of the day

- Left in time to shower and listen to my Praise and Worship music

- Doug's mom had come to live with us so she drove me to the doctor

- Met with the doctor and that's when ... *everything changed*

When Dr. Wonderful looked closely at my port and the 'natural healing' fluid, she said, **"I don't like it and I won't use it."** I thought to myself, **"OH NO! What does that mean?"** I remember even saying out loud, "So I can't get my chemo?" She went on to say that I would need a **PICC** (**P**eripherally **I**nserted **C**entral **C**atheter) until we could figure out what was going on with the port. She suggested that I could try to take my AC/Red Devil Chemo in the vein and that's exactly what I did. She wrote orders to stop using the port and for the Chemo Lab to try to use my vein. Therefore, the infusion was a little slower but I tolerated it well. Thank God. I didn't want to skip a treatment. We were moving right along and I wasn't going to let this delay the treatment schedule.

This chemo hit me about 6:30 PM. Each one was affecting me earlier and earlier. I remembered what my first nurse told me…don't be a hero, just go to bed. I had the same side effects after each chemo except now I had no hair and my eyelashes were beginning to fall out. Somehow, I just hadn't thought about losing my eyelashes. That was very hard. I just lay in bed trying not to move because I did not want to get sick. Doug's mom brought me the anti-nausea medicine and my favorite grape Gatorade.

On February 17, 2009, a **PICC** (a catheter to my heart) was inserted into my right arm. This procedure was completed by a radiologist at the clinic and required no hospitalization or anesthesia even though it is a direct line to my heart. It is very similar to a port except the PICC is outside the body and requires very strict cleaning procedures because of placement. At this point, I was beginning to feel like a pincushion.

Excitement in the Air

Everything was moving right along. The three chemo treatments were behind me, the turbans and wigs were here and as a family, we were adjusting to our new normal. We were literally looking ahead which was easy to do because Paige and her boyfriend Case became **engaged** on February 8, 2009. We had plenty of planning to do to take our minds off of chemo, ports and other cancer related subjects. At home, excitement was in the air. My eldest daughter Paige—my little girl, my nurse—was engaged and she was glowing!

Life was going to get busy, and all would "work together for good" and be accomplished in God's perfect timing.

"And we know that in all things God
works for the good of those who love him,
who have been called according to his purpose."
Romans 8:28 (NIV)

CHEMO MILESTONE

My favorite fuzzy hat

On February 26, 2009, I was back at the Cancer Center for my last **AC/Red Devil Chemo**. I was thrilled! My PICC was inserted in my right arm and this was going to be the first time that it was accessed. First, I met with **Dr. Wonderful** to review my progress. She was surprised that during my last visit I was able to take the AC chemo in the vein and today would be the last AC treatment. YAY! She examined the port site and there was no improvement. In fact, it looked even more suspicious so she was very confident in her decision to not use the port on the last visit. After a review of lab work, I was off to the chemo chair.

The only downside to a **PICC** is the bandage removal each time that it is used. My skin was very thin by this time and if the bandage was ripped off, a layer of skin would come with it. Some nurses were more patient than others. Once the bandage was removed, the site was cleaned and the chemo infusion began. I put my feet up and listened to my Praise and Worship music while I updated my notes regarding my visit.

Routine At Home

When I went home, I ate a light dinner, visited with family a few minutes and went to bed. By the 4th dose of **Red Devil** chemo, more of the drug was in my system and it hit me hard. I took my anti-nausea medicine regularly with my purple Gatorade. I lay very still so I wouldn't get sick. I stayed in bed until midafternoon the next day. I rested Saturday, Sunday and stayed home from work Monday. I usually felt well enough to go to work by Monday but this time was different. I was extremely exhausted, weak and nauseous. Don't be a hero. Just go to bed became my mantra.

I returned to work Tuesday, March 3rd because I needed to prepare the standardized test booklets for the annual spring testing. I worked all week from March 3rd until the following Monday, March 10th.

During that week, I noticed several new symptoms: shortness of breath, extreme exhaustion and a low-grade fever of 99 degrees. Gale, the Instructional Coach, was helping me with testing preparation and she noticed that my breathing had changed. My breathing was labored and every now and then I had to take a deep breath just to catch my breath. I called my doctor's office and the nurse told me that I should be OK as long I didn't have a high fever. I went on working for the entire week and the following Monday, I still had a low-grade fever so I called the doctor. She told me to come in that afternoon.

The Unexpected

When I went to the doctor that afternoon, she was concerned with the redness around my port site and that I had been running a fever for a week. She put me on immediate bed rest. I told her that I had standardized testing that week and she said, "I don't care. You don't go back to work until I tell you that you can go back to work." OH MY! This was a major roadblock! I called the principal to tell her what had happened and I apologized profusely. Then I was sent to the chemo lab for IV antibiotics because they were supposed to work faster than the pills.

The next day, my mother-in-law went out of town with some friends. I told her that I would be fine yet in all honesty I did not feel well at all. I could barely breathe and I hurt all over. I ate popsicles and stayed hydrated with purple Gatorade. By mid-afternoon, my fever was getting higher. I went to the chemo lab for my IV antibiotics and my fever was 101 degrees. It was definitely getting worse. The chemo lab nurses had to report my condition to **Dr. Wonderful** and well—she sent me to the hospital. I called Doug and my mom and told them that I was being admitted to the hospital. Even though I didn't want to go to the hospital, I loved my doctor. That's why I call her **Dr. Wonderful** because she was so smart. She suspected all along that the port was in-fected and that is why she refused to use it. She ad-mitted me to the hospital because she was concerned that the infection would lead to **Sepsis**, a potentially life threatening complication from an infection that could spread through the bloodstream.

I stayed in the hospital seven long nights and six even longer days. No wigs: just my fuzzy hat, mini-mal makeup, and occasionally I would get dressed and sit up in a chair. My dearest friends and members of my support team visited me and for the first time saw me in my fuzzy hat because I didn't have my wig collection close by. By Friday, I really wanted to go home for the weekend but **Dr. Wonderful** said, **"NO!"** I had to stay the weekend and on Monday, March 16, 2009 that infected port was removed from my chest by the Breast Surgeon. The surgeon had to take several inches of the surrounding skin so that she could ensure that the infected skin would be gone. I came through all of this with an ugly scar but I am alive. I was released from the hospital that night and I went back to work the next day.

I was **half way** finished with chemo! Woo hoo!

GOOD NEWS...AT LAST

Back to Work

After a week in the hospital and more rest than I had in years, I was back at work on Tuesday, March 17, 2009. I wanted my next chemo treatment that week but **Dr. Wonderful** made me wait until the following week. By the time Monday, March 23rd arrived, I was ready to get started with the next four treatments. I still followed the same routine to schedule my appointment late in the day, shower and listen to my Praise and Worship music. Doug's mom, Sharon, drove me because I would be given Benadryl with the Taxol chemo. I didn't know what else to expect from this new chemo: **Taxol (Paclitaxel)** and **Herceptin.**

   Dr. Wonderful was glad to see me doing well. It was during this visit that she told me she always suspected my port was infected and she was very thankful we didn't use the port. I could have gotten the infection in my blood. She went on to tell me that I was **BRCA** negative and that was HUGE news. Therefore, I did not carry or pass the breast cancer gene to my girls. That was a positive! My white cell counts were good and I no longer needed the Neupogen shots. YAY! I was thrilled. After she examined me, she had more good news. The large tumor in the right axilla was probably about half of the original size and the tumor in the right breast was shrinking as well. From now on, I would need to come to the Chemo Lab weekly. One week I would receive Taxol and Herceptin and on alternating weeks I would receive **only Herceptin**. The best news was that I could drive myself to those appointments (Herceptin). YES!!

Finding the Positive

After the great visit with Dr. Wonderful, I was ready to get this treatment underway. Taxol and Herceptin would take about three hours. Sometimes Doug's mom would go to get us McDonald's cheeseburgers to eat before the Benadryl kicked in. Plus, it helped pass the time for her. I would have to update my notebook quickly because the Benadryl would make me go right to sleep, so the time passed quickly for me. We came home and everything was normal. I thought to myself, 'This one was going to be much easier.' I got up and got dressed for work the next day, Tuesday and Wednesday. Both of those days were normal work days. I went to work Thursday and that's when it hit me. I started to ache/hurt all over at about 11 AM. Doug came and picked me up about two hours later and I went home and went straight to bed. I remembered my motto: If I was hurting, then the chemo was working! As a result of this pain, I knew pain was good when the chemo was working. I always tried to **find a positive** in the journey.

FUNNY THINGS THAT HAPPENED ON THE WAY TO A CURE

It was now late March and I was feeling great. Spring break was here which meant a week of vacation from work and surprisingly I only had two appointments that week. I drove myself to chemo and wore my fuzzy hat because I didn't want to put on a wig that day. I wanted to be comfortable. After chemo, I went to Michaels craft store looking for an idea to help organize and save all of the cards that I had received since my diagnosis. I totally forgot about doctor's orders not to go to the store. OOPS!

Leaving Memories for My Girls

In January as people began to find out about my diagnosis, I was inundated with cards. It was such a blessing. I dated each card and put them in a basket. Now the basket was overflowing. People began sending cards, emails, letters and handwritten notes. As I walked around Michaels, I found a scrapbook that was perfect. It was very plain, no plastic sheet covers or leather binders…just basic. I chose one album and then I went to pick out some background paper. One thing led to another and I ended up with scrap booking paper, prints and solids, cute stickers and jeweled stickers that were words of encouragement.

When I got home, I began my project. First, I glued the background paper on the page and then glued the cards down. All of my January cards filled the first album. Highly emotional and full of gratitude, I just cried. To think that so many people took the time to reach out to me brought me tears of joy. As I looked at the pages I filled in the empty spots with the stickers I had purchased, which were words of encouragement. I went back to Michaels the next day and bought three more books so that I would have the same style of book to continue this project.

This was a fun way to record my journey and it became very therapeutic as I took time to read each card as I placed it in the album. In addition, I wanted my girls to have something from my journey because I didn't know what the future would hold. You can see from the pictures that the January book has a cute ribbon to hold it closed and the other books don't. I had to keep it simple.

Fuzzy Hat Stares

Did I mention that I was in Michaels wearing my fuzzy hat? I surprised myself by wearing it in public. I got a few looks, a few avoidance moves but I just smiled and walked with confidence. I was grateful to be feeling so good and driving myself that I didn't care about my **fuzzy hat stares**.

The **main victory** in all of this was having the **courage** to go to the store in my fuzzy hat.

CELEBRATING KELSEY

Spring break was over and it was back to reality. The second dose of **Taxol** and **Herceptin** was scheduled for April 7th, the first Tuesday back at school. This time, I was prepared to ask the doctor for pain medication. I was trying to work through chemo but I knew I didn't need to prove how brave I was, so I got my pain meds. There was no nausea with Taxol, for me at least, but the body pain was **indescribable**. The only way that I can think to explain it is that every cell in my skin hurt and it felt like someone was peeling my skin off.

I tried to change my chemo treatments to Wednesdays so the side effects wouldn't kick in until Saturdays but **Dr. Wonderful** could only move it from Mondays to Tuesdays because I was already off of the schedule due to the unexpected week in the hospital.

Honoring Kelsey

After chemo, I went home and got ready to go to the High School Hall of Fame Induction Ceremony where they were honoring the top 20 students in the senior class for highest grade point averages (GPA). Our youngest daughter, Kelsey, was being recognized for graduating **fifth** in a senior class of approximately 450 students. Super amazing!! She was taking five Advanced Placement (AP) classes, helping around the house and dealing with my illness. She was so brave and never told me all that she was going through until five years later when I asked her to journal how she felt during that period in our lives. I never realized the toll it took on her. I was so thankful to be able to attend the award ceremonies. Doug and I sat in the back right corner of the high school auditorium. I couldn't be more proud. That night we celebrated Kelsey.

HE KNOWS MY NAME

I was between my sixth and seventh chemo treatment. Only two more to go. The sixth chemo treatment hit me hard. Every muscle and cell in my body hurt. At the last appointment, **Dr. Wonderful** told me to sit outside in the late afternoon to get some vitamin D and it would be good for me. So, I decided to sit outside for a while. It was just the squirrels and me in the backyard. I was looking at the aloe plants because that was the only place in the backyard that gets the sun.

A Moment of Weakness

It had been a hard weekend. I was home from a long day of work, and I just lost it. **Finally, I broke down and began to list all of the challenges that had come my way since December.** I listed everything for God, as if He didn't know. It went like this:

- Cancer, God?

- Stage 3a

- Grade III, aggressive

- Chemo
- I have no hair
- My eyelashes and eyebrows are gone
- I hurt all over
- My port got infected
- A week in the hospital
- Neupogen shots
- A PICC line
- Needle after needle after needle after needle

I said, "I don't understand why you let this happen to me. I'm sorry God. I know I'm not supposed to question you but I'm your child. Why? Why did you let this happen to me?"

Then I felt bad. You may read this and think that I was wrong to ever talk to God that way. I will say that God already knew what I was thinking. He's God. I knew that I couldn't stay in that state of mind so I started finding the positive things about my situation. I made a list of all the things I was thankful for:

- My team of doctors
- The chemo I could receive
- **Herceptin** for the fact I could still work
- Kelsey's successful senior year

- Paige because she could give me the **Neupogen** shots

- My caregivers: Doug, Doug's mom and my mom

I knew in my **head** that God worked all things for my good; I just didn't **feel** it at the time. In fact, I felt all alone.

With tears running down my face, I asked God to be with me and wrap His arms around me like he promised that he would do in His word. I was broken…I sat in silence…

Renewal of the Soul

Along came a beautiful hummingbird, and then his mate arrived a couple of minutes later. They fluttered around the aloe plants and obtained the nectar from the aloe bloom. We had lived at that house 14 years and I had worked in the yard at all times of the day and I had never seen a hummingbird, much less a pair of hummingbirds. Then, I remembered a verse in the Bible about God taking care of the birds of the air.

> *"Look at the birds of the air;*
> *they do not sow or reap or store away in barns,*
> *and yet your heavenly Father feeds them.*
> *Are you not much more valuable than they?"*
> Matthew 6:26 (NIV)

I sat in silence once again but this time it was a good silence. This was the kind of silence and time with God that renews your soul. I knew God had my back in all of this. I knew God was in control. I went inside and began to review notes in my devotional book. I read the notes from the Sunday that I was in the hospital, March 15th. In those notes was a phrase…**"I know God remembers me."** In fact, that phrase is listed 73 times in the Bible in reference to God taking care of us. Then, I listened to my favorite Praise and Worship song, *"He Knows My Name"* by Tommy Walker. Here are the words to the first verse/chorus:

> *I have a Maker*
> *He formed my heart,*
> *before even time began*
> *My life was in His hands*
> *He knows my name*
> *He knows my every thought,*

He sees each tear that falls
and hears me when I call

God, remembered me all along. I just needed to return to the source of strength.

ALWAYS HOPEFUL

> "...even when you cannot see Him right now and cannot understand what He is doing, you know Him."
>
> My Utmost For His Highest

My spirit had been renewed by spending quiet time with God and by the visit from the hummingbirds. I only saw the tiny birds one more time after that day and haven't seen them since. I was moving on to finish my debilitating chemo by May 5th, and then on to surgery.

Final Two Chemotherapy Treatments

I made it through my seventh chemo on April 21st and my eighth and **LAST** chemo on May 5th. I had the same routine where I saw **Dr. Wonderful** first and then off to the chemo lab. My appointments were still on Tuesdays and I tried to work the rest of the week. By Friday, I needed my pain medication. By the time I was near the end of my chemo, Doug drove me to work most Mondays and Fridays. I was physically weak and exhausted but I made myself go to work because I wanted to keep the same routine. My last **Taxol/Herceptin** chemo was on May 5th. I continued to go to the chemo lab weekly for Herceptin.

Preparing My Body for Surgery

At the last two appointments with **Dr. Wonderful,** I was given specific directions to begin taking B6, B12, Vitamin E w/o Selenium, Calcium and Vitamin D in order to build my immune system. My vitamin D levels were very low and they needed to increase before I could start radiation. Over the next 9 months, I would need an Echocardiogram every 3 months because Herceptin could damage my heart.

After a final consultation with my team of doctors, Breast Surgeon, Plastic Surgeon and Dr. Wonderful, I decided to have the following procedures:

• Partial bilateral mastectomy, to include lumpectomy

• Lymph node dissection, right side

• Port insertion, at which time the PICC would be removed

The surgery was set for June 3, 2009. There was no negotiation even though that was the last week of the school year. *Really?* ***The last week of the school year is the busiest week!*** The surgery needed to take place in a timely manner. I had to remind myself that my health was MORE important than the job.

Preparing My Mind and Soul for Surgery

My morning devotion on May 8th, three days after my last chemo, was just what I needed at the time.

From My Utmost For His Highest, by Oswald Chambers

"Entrust yourself to God's hands. Is there something in your life for which you need perseverance right now? Maintain your intimate relationship with Jesus Christ through perseverance of faith. Proclaim as Job did, 'Though He slay me, yet will I trust Him.' (Job 13:15) ...even when you cannot see Him right now and cannot understand what He is doing, you know Him."

Those were powerful words of encouragement because I didn't understand why I was in this situation.

I **KNEW GOD** was with me every day.

GRADUATION CELEBRATION WEEK

I was going to the chemo lab for weekly Herceptin infusions since I could drive myself and schedule the treatments after work. I had three weeks to regain my strength before Kelsey's graduation week.

Graduation Week was very busy:

- Tuesday, May 26 – Baccalaureate Service

- Wednesday, May 27 – Cheri, my sister-in-law, arrived from New Mexico

- Thursday, May 28– Senior Awards

- Friday, May 29 – Graduation Ceremony

- Sunday, May 31 – Kelsey's Graduation Party

At the Senior Awards, Kelsey received multiple honors:

- Polk Education Foundation Scholarship

- National Honor Society Achievement Award

- Certificate of Academic Excellence from the Science Department

- The American Legion Award

WOW! We were all very surprised. The Science Award was a unanimous election by all of the teachers in the Science department, which was a major accomplishment. Also, she was chosen for the American Legion Award because she possessed high qualities of courage, honor, leadership, patriotism, scholarship and service. She was having a great culmination to her senior year. She was on her way to the college of her dreams: The University of Florida. We were so very proud and happy for her.

On Sunday afternoon, friends and family gathered at our house to celebrate Kelsey. Friends, former teachers and family came from near and far. She was overwhelmed by the show of support. The house was full of friends, family, laughter and support. **It had been a long time since these sounds filled our home.** The party would not have been a success without help from my sister-in-law, Cheri. She is the ultimate party planner and she worked her magic to make it a special day for all of us.

Kelsey
From a Brave to a Gator
cake decorated in high school colors and college colors

Now the focus would turn to my surgery, which was scheduled for Wednesday, June 3, 2009.

AN UNBELIEVABLE REPORT AND CELEBRATION

A few days before my surgery, the breast surgeon ordered an ultrasound of my right breast and right axilla so she could know the progress I had made with chemotherapy. I went to the Women's Center and sat down until it was my turn. When I was called, I changed into the robe and sat in the next waiting room. All of the ladies sat there awkwardly and tried not to stare at each other. Then my name was called and I walked down the hall to another waiting room. One thing I have learned through all of these medical appointments is that you **hurry up** to **wait**.

Finally, I was called to the room where the ultrasound would take place. I recognized the technician. She was the one who was guiding the ultrasound machine during my biopsy. I lay down on the table and she began the ultrasound of the right breast, snapping pictures rapidly and then on to the right axilla where she took even more pictures.

Our conversation went like this:

Tech: "You must have had some good chemo."

Me: "Chemo AND prayer!"

Tech: "Yeah, that positive thinking, meditation and prayer stuff works to help people remain positive through this."

....and she walked out of the room to talk to the doctor

Doctor: "Do you remember us? We did your biopsy."

Me: "Yes, I remember you."

Doctor: "You have made good progress. Your tumors were very large and they have significantly changed."

Me: "I believe in prayer and miracles."

The doctor just looked at me and finished writing her notes. They both left the room and I got dressed.

My Response

When I got to my car, I just sat there and cried tears of joy. Just a few weeks ago I was fussing at God for having to go through this and now I was over-whelmed with thankfulness. I was not deserving of His grace. I called Doug and told him the good news and explained that I was crying tears of joy. I sat there at least 10 minutes to regain my composure. God is so good!

I KNEW that I would have good results from the surgery and this was just the confirmation that I needed.

SURPRISE! Celebration!

As I drove to work, I mentally prepared myself for the emotions of the last day before I left for surgery. In less than 24 hours, I would endure six hours of surgery that would require three specialists. I received the great news from the ultrasound but only Doug and I knew about that report because we wanted to wait until after the surgery. On this day, I focused my positivity to reflect on just how grateful I was for the staff at school. I wrote the staff a letter so that I would not need to say any goodbyes for the summer break. I was not pleased to miss the last three days of school, but I knew better than to argue with doctors.

Ever since the staff found out about my diagnosis when they returned to school in January of 2009, they continued to support me. The first time I wore a wig I was so self-conscious and they acted like it was no big deal. When I had to wear my favorite fuzzy hat to work, they made me feel accepted. They provided meals every Thursday for at least five months and my family looked forward to Thursdays. It was a much needed night off for the caregivers not to worry about food. Every now and then, grade levels and individuals would give me care packets, gift cards and cards of encouragement. They loved me through those difficult months and always treated me kindly.

When I got to school, I noticed one pink shirt, three pink shirts, and grade levels of pink shirts … until I eventually realized that all of the staff wore pink shirts on my last day. It still brings me to tears six years later as I write this book. I was surrounded by support and kindness every day.

After school was out the principal told me that she needed me to go with her to the Computer Lab. She was quite convincing, so off we went. We did go to the Computer Lab and walked straight through to the back door of the Media Center where the entire staff had gathered and made a tunnel of pink to welcome me as I entered the room. When I came to the school years before, I brought a special tradition with me. On the last day of school, I would have the staff gathered to make a tunnel for the last bus students to walk through as they boarded the bus. The students always loved it. Needless to say, I was so overwhelmed. As I looked around the room, there was a sea of pink. The staff was wearing pink shirts, holding pink balloons and wearing surgical masks. It was an amazing show of support.

My birthday is in July so we gathered to celebrate an early birthday featuring my favorite colors: pink and yellow. They arranged for me to have a month of birthdays so that I would have a card to open every day during my recovery from surgery. They also made a money ribbon because they knew I hadn't been able to go to the beach during chemo and that was and still is one of my favorite places to relax. Kindness, gratitude, compassion and joy surrounded me that day.

A journey through breast cancer or any other illness changes you. You can allow it to change you for the good or you can become bitter. It's not easy! Healing takes time. Believe me…CANCER SUCKS, but life goes on and happiness is a choice.

I choose to be happy every day and I choose to SMILE!

GET THAT CANCER OUT!

Five months had passed and I made it through chemotherapy. It had been a busy time full of school events for my youngest daughter and a few plans here and there for Paige's wedding. This incredibly important day began with keeping our routines normal. Kelsey went to school and Paige went to work. I wanted to continue that sense of normalcy that we had worked so hard to maintain.

First Stop ... Women's Center

At last, the day had come...surgery day. Doug drove me to the Women's Center to have a procedure known as: **Pre-Operative Needle Localization**. In order to locate the tumor, a mammography technologist and radiologists secured my right breast in the mammogram machine using a special piece of equipment to hold my breast in place. That part did not hurt like a mammogram. It was imperative that I hold still. Next the radiologists positioned a needle in my breast, which was used to locate the tumor. The video screen guided the location of the needle. The tumor was marked with a metal clip during the biopsy, which made it easier to locate. Two pictures were taken to ensure that the needle was positioned at the point of the clip. Yay! Success on the first try. Then, a wire was inserted through the needle and the needle was removed. Two more pictures were taken to ensure that the wire was at the point of the metal clip. Woo hoo! Success two times in a row.

Off to the Surgery Center

The technician put a surgical gown on me, so as not to disturb the wire and I was ushered out of the back door of the Women's Center and into the car. I arrived at the Surgery Center in that lovely surgical gown with a wire sticking out of my right breast. The wire that I was not to move at all. I was shown to a room that reminded me of a 6×6 box. A nurse entered the room and began to ask me all of the usual pre-operative questions: medications, allergies, etc.... then she asked me, "Why are you here today?" I began the list:

• **Lumpectomy right breast** (Removal of cancer to be combined with the partial bilateral mastectomy on the right side).

• **Partial Bilateral Mastectomy** (Removal of part of both breasts)

- **Lymph Node Dissection** – Right Axilla, (removal of lymph nodes)
- **Port Insertion** – (2nd attempt to insert a chemo port in the upper left side of chest)

WOW! After five long months, I could rattle off all of those medical terms with ease. I had become a very informed advocate for my own health.

Holding Pen

After a few minutes, I was walked back to the waiting area, which I refer to as a holding pen, where the nurses started the I.V. and asked me all of the same questions I just answered for the first nurse. I sat totally naked except for the thin surgical gown covering my body, with a perfect stranger seated across from me, staring at me until I felt completely uncomfortable. Can you tell how I feel about the holding pen? It reminds me of the SPCA!

Both doctors (the breast surgeon and plastic surgeon), came by to talk to me and reviewed how each procedure would take place. Then the anesthesiologist came by. I told him to make sure that he gave me plenty of anti-nausea medicine because with past procedures, nausea was a problem. Doug was the only one allowed to wait with me in the holding pen until they took me back for surgery. My mom, Uncle Leon (from Ohio), mother-in-law and sister-in-law (from

New Mexico) were all waiting in the lobby. My sister-in-law had come for Kelsey's graduation and just happened to be able to stay for the surgery.

Here We Go!

It was my turn. Doug kissed me before I went back to the operating room. As I was on my way to my special room, all I could think of was, "Please God, let them get it all, whatever it takes." I also said a prayer of forgiveness and prayed for every member of my family.

The breast surgeon previously explained that she would work simultaneously with the plastic surgeon during my procedure. There would be three incisions in each breast. They would start with the right breast. Locate the tumor and remove all surrounding tissue and all tissue in front of the tumor, similar to a breast reduction. The plastic surgeon would put the right breast back together and then she would do her best to make the left side the same size so that they would be symmetrical. They would also place drains in the surgical sites, one on each side, to allow fluid to drain. The drain was inserted through a one-inch incision site and held in place by stitches.

After the breast surgery was completed, the breast surgeon made a three-inch incision, cutting through tendons and muscle under my arm, right axilla. Her goal was to remove as many lymph nodes as she could. Next, would be the port insertion. She used the same incision site as the last one where the infected port was removed in March. **Six hours later**, everything was completed and my upper body was wrapped like a mummy, holding the drains in place and I was sent to recovery.

Recovery

I gave clear instructions that after the surgery, my fuzzy hat was to be put on my head before Doug was allowed back to the recovery room. I'm not sure that happened. I do know that when I began to wake up, Doug was there and my fuzzy hat was on. He sat with me patiently as I tried my best to wake up and get out of there. They made me drink some Sprite. I was feeling good and I almost dressed myself. The cancer that tried to kill me was finally cut out of my body and I was alive!

I walked out of the surgery center with 10 incisions in my upper body and too many stitches to count! I had a pain pump and medicine for the nausea. When I needed meds, I took my meds. I again remembered what Jerry, my first chemo nurse, told me: "Don't be a hero." I slept most of that day and remember my sister-in-law the next morning telling me that she wished she could stay and take care of me but she had to leave. Doug drove her to the airport and his mom left a couple of days later. Doug, my girls, and my mom took care of me the first week. In a week, we would find out the results on the medical report from the surgeon.

I stood in faith and upon God's word that I would **live** and not die.

MY MIRACLE

My first week of recovery went well. Victory Church, my home church, provided delicious meals the week after surgery and that was a great blessing. Doug, my girls, and my mom took turns checking on me.

Post-Operative Visit

My post-op visit was scheduled approximately one week after my surgery. During that visit, I saw the plastic surgeon and the breast surgeon. First, the plastic surgeon's nurse removed the mummy bandages. Then the plastic surgeon examined eight of the 10 incisions. Everything looked good so the nurse removed a few stitches, which wasn't the most pleasant experience but all in all, I was making great progress. Then the pain pump was removed.

Next, the breast surgeon came in to examine me. She looked at the incisions and focused on the right axilla. She asked me to lift my arm as high as I could so I hesitantly lifted my arm about half way in the air. Then she took my arm and pulled it straight up. I just knew my stitches were going to burst but they didn't. She gave me some exercises to do every day to help me regain full range of motion.

Pathology Report: Complete Response to Chemo

Then she began to explain the pathology report. From the right axilla, she removed all lymph nodes that she could see and reach. Below is a summary of the conversation:

Dr.: "I didn't find anything."

Me: "You didn't get the cancer?"

Dr.: "It was gone."

Me: "What do you mean?"

Dr.: "I removed 20+ lymph nodes and there were two that were necrotic." "They were the size of a regular lymph node."

Me: "I don't understand."

Dr.: "I found the two lymph nodes that were tagged during the biopsy but the cancer cells were dead and the lymph nodes were the size of a normal lymph node."

First, in case you have forgotten, when I was diagnosed there were two tumors in the right axilla. One was the size of a 9 volt battery and the other one was the size of 1/2 of an AA battery. Now, they not only contained dead cells but they were the size of a normal lymph node, which was a significant change.

The news really didn't register with me at that time. My **Dr. Wonderful** refers to it as a '**complete response to chemo**'. Every time a doctor says that, I echo, "...or a **miracle**." Some doctors give me a smile and others remain stoic.

One More Surgery

Next, the breast surgeon explained the results from the lumpectomy/reduction of the right breast. The tumor in the right breast was busted into small pieces. The pathology report reflected that it looked like buckshot in the tissue, scattered everywhere. They were just the size of little pencil dots. So there was no lump to remove. I am still amazed at the outcome. However, the pathology report did not confirm that there was a clear margin of healthy tissue so I needed an additional surgery known as a 'margin revision.'

The surgical drains remained in place and the nurse wrapped me in a garment similar to a tube top except it had to be very snug to hold the drains in place. Doug and I went home and processed all of that information. Now I realize why the ultrasound technician was shocked with my progress. It was a truly unbelievable response.

It was MY MIRACLE.

JUST ONE MORE SURGERY

About the time I hoped to return to work part time, I was scheduled for a surgery known as a margin revision. In my post-op visit, the breast surgeon explained that there was one cancerous spot on the border of the clean tissue. The goal of the surgery is to leave a margin of at least 1mm of normal, cancer free tissue.

I arrived at the Surgery Center at 7:00 AM on June 16th. I went through the usual details: financial responsibilities, and then back to the **holding pen** where I changed my clothes and got ready. I asked the nurse to pull the curtain so everybody couldn't stare at me. I was hoping that the surgeon would take the drains out during the surgery. The breast surgeon stopped by to see me and reassured me that she was going to get clear margins. She previously asked me if a pathologist could attend the surgery. She confirmed that the pathologist would be attending the surgery and would be able to examine the tissue immediately to ensure the cancer cells were removed. I would need to wait for the pathology tissue samples to be analyzed before I received an official report. The breast surgeon would gain access through the 3 incisions in the right breast from the surgery on June 3rd. She explained that the plastic surgeon could not be there and she would do her best to put me back together. The anesthesiologist also stopped by. I told him I had past issues with nausea after surgery. He assured me that he would give me something to prevent unnecessary nausea.

I was ready to go back for the procedure. Doug kissed me goodbye. This time it was just Doug in the lobby because this was supposed to be a shorter, uncomplicated surgery. The nurse took me back to the operating room where everyone greeted me and made introductions. The surgeon came in and I told her, "Let's do this."

The next thing I remember was that I was in the recovery area. I was trying to wake up but it wasn't working. I could hear the nurse asking Doug if I opened my eyes yet. The nurse kept saying, "Okay Laura. It's done." The nurse told the doctor, as she came by, that I wasn't awake yet. They were standing at my bed and I could hear them but I could not respond. Neither could I open my eyes. I could hear her talking to me and about me, but I couldn't move. I wasn't scared, though. I did tell God that if this was my time to go that I would be okay with it as long as … I was going to heaven. (Obviously, I didn't speak that but I was praying silently.)

Later, the surgeon came by again. I heard the nurse and doctor talking about my vital signs. They looked good so the doctor said to give me time. I was trying to open my eyes and they all told me to relax and take my time. They assured me that I was okay. The doctor completed another surgery and came by to check on me. This time I opened my eyes a little and gave her a half smile.

How ironic! After the six-hour surgery on June 3rd, I was in recovery 30-40 minutes. This surgery was supposed to be so easy (1 hour) and yet I was in recovery 2-3 hours. Eventually, I **walked** out of the surgical center and went home to bed.

At the post-op visit, the surgeon gave me great news that the pathology report was clear. The surgical tubes had to stay in place until the drainage slowed down. I started Herceptin again, the good chemo, one week later.

Plans for Paige's wedding would begin soon and we had only a few weeks to plan the entire wedding.

WE DANCED IN THE RAIN

The dress

Wedding Plans Begin

While Paige's engagement had been a very exciting and welcome distraction in the middle of the chaos, now it was time to get busy. I was not working due to the surgeries and Paige had a few days off from work. We were determined to plan the wedding.

Paige found a dress in the spring so that important task was complete. All she needed to do now was to arrange for alterations. Our days were filled with fun activities because she was getting married in January 2010. She selected navy and white for her wedding colors. We added a splash of silver to the invitations and the wedding favors, just like a silver lining in all of this chaos.

The challenge at our church was to find a venue large enough for 300 guests. The maximum capacity of the wedding chapel was 300. The guest lists needed to be adjusted to meet that number. We made several phone calls and talked to many friends for recommendations for flowers, photographers and invitations. After we narrowed down our list, we began to schedule appointments.

In three days, we visited and secured the chapel, the reception venue, a florist, linens, invitations, a photographer and the cake. Deposits were made and all we had left to do was to work on the other details: favors, music, programs and menu cards.

Road Trip

The most memorable trip was when Paige drove me 67 miles to the company that would supply and set up the linens. With surgical drains in place and the special wrap that resembled a tight tube top to hold the drains in place, I gingerly got in and out of her car. I put on my make up and favorite wig and we set out to find the linens distributor. We entered the address in the GPS and off we went. It began to rain so hard that we could barely see the road and it felt like Paige hit every pothole on the road. With each bump, I had pain in each side where the surgical drains were held by a couple of stitches. We got lost, we laughed and had the best time. Eventually, we found the linen vendor and walked the muddy path to the door. We were able to make all of the arrangements in one trip and as we left, the joy of the occasion washed over us and we danced in the rain, stitches, tubes and all.

Life isn't about waiting for the storm to pass…
It's about learning to dance in the rain.
–Anonymous

JULY...A WONDERFUL TIME

The surgical tubes were finally removed on July 1st. To put it in perspective, my first surgery was June 3rd, and my second surgery, the margin revision, was June 16th. So for almost a month, I lived with unwieldy, annoying tubes coming out of my rib cage on each side. I was so glad to be done with the tubes! Goodbye tubes...Hello radiation! During July 2009, I continued Herceptin weekly and asked to be changed to a treatment plan of once every three weeks because I would return to school at the end of July. As an Assistant Principal, I had responsibilities during the summer and I had to officially report to work a couple of weeks before the teachers. In that time, I had to prepare schedules, revise class lists and ensure the school was ready for the new school year.

Kelsey Leaves for The University of Florida

This month was full of preparation to send Kelsey, our youngest daughter, off to college. She was preparing to join the Gator Nation at The University of Florida (UF) in August 2009. In retrospect, this was the last month that we were all in the same house as a family unit and yet excitement for the girls' future was the focus.

There were so many details to take care of. The suggested list of items arrived from the University and Kelsey was excited to decorate her dorm room. It began: linens, matching pillows, bathroom necessities, TV, microwave, bike, helmet and that didn't even include her schedule and books. It was busy.

Kelsey at UF Orientation...Go Gators!

Radiation

I met with the radiologist who was also a female doctor along with all the doctors on my team. As she reviewed my chart, she said something along the lines of, "You should do well. You had a 'complete response to chemo" to which I replied, "I call it my miracle." She smiled politely and went on to explain to me that that's when the chemotherapy completely attacks the cancer cells. Then we discussed the radiation plan. I would have 35 rounds of radiation. That ends up to be 7 weeks, 5 times a week, give or take a holiday with the center closed.

I was scheduled for radiotherapy, which is the treatment of the disease with radiation. At that appointment I got two small pencil dot tattoos. Those markings would be used to line me up under the machine so that the radiation would most effectively target the right area. The next day, I came back for a walk-through so that the technicians could set the machines and the following day radiation began. I will admit that I was frightened of the unknown. For example: how do they know they are only radiating the exact area? What if I sneeze, is it going to zap my eye? The machine was enormous. Part of it had a moving part that the technician lined up according to my new tattoos. The technician left the room every time, so what would happen if she bumped something on the way out of the room and the radiation missed the spot? I had many thoughts going through my mind. I prayed continuously for strength and complete healing.

Once the preliminary visits were completed, it took me longer to drive there than it did to receive the treatment. I had returned to working full-time. The

Cancer Center scheduled me at 6 AM or 6 PM. I drove myself to and from radiation. If it was the early morning appointment, I went straight to work from radiation. I would joke every now and then that I was 'glowing' to ease the awkwardness in the office. When I was about ¾ of the way into treatment, I started to get sensitive skin but they gave me some cream and it was not a significant problem. I was a little tired but as a school administrator in August and September, fatigue it is to be expected. I could not differentiate if the exhaustion was caused by radiation or my 10-hour workdays. I just kept going...one day at a time.

People always ask me: How did you do it? How did you work through chemo, port complications and radiation? My answer is...I was not alone. I have a personal relationship with the 'Great Physician' who is God. I trusted God to direct my doctors and to give me strength.

Long before cancer my life verse was *Jeremiah 29:11: 'I know what I am doing. I have it all planned out—plans to take care of you, not abandon you, plans to give you the future you HOPE for.'* (MSG)

RADIATION IS OVER...
SO NOW WHAT?

ACCEPT WHAT IS.
LET GO OF WHAT WAS.
HAVE FAITH IN
WHAT WILL BE.
LAURASJOURNEYOFHOPE.COM

By the time I was scheduled to see **Dr. Wonderful**, radiation was over and I had come through it with minimal side effects.

What's next?

Dr. Wonderful immediately started me on a chemo pill, Arimidex. The initial plan was to take it for five years as long as my bones, bone density and joints would allow.

Arimidex (Anastrozole) is a type of hormone therapy known as an Aromatase Inhibitor. How does Anastrozole work? Breast cancer is stimulated to grow by female hormones: estrogen and progesterone. Anastrozole (Arimidex) works to block the effects of the female hormones.

This is the way I have come to think about breast cancer. The very hormone, estrogen, that defines you as a woman, ends up globbing together with other estrogen cells to become breast cancer. So the very hormone that makes you a woman, tries to kill you. I hope you can infer that I find this entire concept hideous, outrageous and unacceptable. **However, I can't change that so I will only give it this small paragraph.**

I started Arimidex in October of 2009 and I was a trooper. I kept taking it even though it took a toll on my body:

• By the end of the 12-hour workday, I could barely walk.

• By Friday or Saturday, I hurt so bad that I could literally feel pain from every cell in my skin and it hurt.

• It felt like someone was peeling my skin off.

With that said, I would take to the couch with my pain meds and heating pad.

Actually, compared to others, my symptoms were minimal. Four years into the medication, I spoke to Dr. Wonderful and she switched me to Femara in October of 2013. Femara is in the same category of medicine. Its purpose is to block estrogen. Even though October 2014 was my 5-year point, I still take Femara. As long as it doesn't affect my bone density, joints and ability to function, I will take it.

I am blessed because I was diagnosed with Estrogen Receptor-Positive (ER+) breast cancer so I have an additional chemo pill to block that estrogen. I am too blessed to be stressed! I'm alive so it's a good day!

CAREGIVERS NEED CARE

My definition of the caregiver...

A person who:

• Changes his/her work schedule to drive you to chemo

• Ensures you take your anti-nausea medicine when you are so sick from chemo/surgery that you just don't care

• Ensures you eat a little protein when you can't taste a thing because protein rebuilds cells

- Sits hours upon hours at doctor's appointments, chemo labs, hospitals and pharmacies

- Prepares meals for your family when you can't

- Stands by when you have to make a trip to the bathroom to make sure you don't pass out or start heaving your guts up

- Gives you Neupogen shots at home (Thank God my daughter became a nurse a few days before my diagnosis)

- Greets guests with a smile while you put your wig on

- Thanks visitors for the food and explains that you just can't see them today

- Moves from out-of-state to stay with you as long as possible (mother-in-law)

- Pretends to never see your bald head because you would just cry if you knew the truth

- Gives up softball because of the need at home, even though a scholarship is possible (my youngest daughter in her senior year)

- Buys groceries because you are not allowed to go to the store; assumes the coordination of all school functions

- Cleans the house, folds laundry, does dishes...when you can't

• Watches you go through 'hell' and tells you that you look great

• Sprays Lysol in your office every day when you leave to be sure it is germ free

• Makes pink curtains for your office

• Holds a Pink Celebration when you need the support of friends and colleagues

Caregivers need to have someone to talk to when they feel overwhelmed. They need plenty of rest, a break now and then and to have an outlet or join a support group, if possible. For example:

• If a husband is caring for his wife, his buddies need to take him out for a guys night, football game or just get away for a few hours

• If a wife is caring for her husband, her friends need to plan a girls night out

• The same if a parent is caring for a child…aunts, uncles, and friends need to come over and take turns so that the primary caregiver can have a break

I wanted my close family members to write and share how they felt during this part of our lives. I hope you find their statements helpful.

A Husband as a Caregiver

Cancer – When we first heard the news, the one thing I remember is that my oldest daughter (21) came to me and asked: When is mommy going to die? During this time when we heard the "C" word, it was a death sentence. Although we were a strong, faith filled family we believed that God was in control of everything in our life, for some reason it seemed that Cancer was something outside of that layer of faith.

There were times I encountered different people that had this disease and I remember laying hands on them and praying for them. But now that the disease was in our life, for some reason it was harder to find the faith I had praying and believing for others.

Through this experience I learned more about my faith and myself than I would have never known without this encounter. I used to think I knew what people went through but I had no idea. Looking back I see that the caregivers go through a different emotional experience than the one that has the actual disease.

Cancer is something that brings all the different emotions out of your spouse. Although her faith was strong there were times that she showed her real feelings. Being the husband, you are the one person on this earth that she can confide in. Of course she tries to never show this side of herself to anyone else; to the outside world she tries to be strong and brave.

I would have different people come to me and ask how your wife is doing, which you would expect. That would have been my question but now I add, how are you also doing? Just remember that Cancer has a major impact on everyone in the family and it changes your life. It is up to you if this change is negative or positive.

Trying to carry the load of all the different family issues that needed to be completed along with my work responsibilities created an overwhelming state of mind at times. This is such a difficult time and if you let it, it will consume your thoughts and pull you down. Stay as positive as you can, if you start thinking about all the negatives you start asking why and then the blame game starts. As men we have the tendency to try and figure everything out and if you get caught up into this process it will show in your attitude. Your life will also change and your responsibilities as a husband will expand into areas that you are not used to. As the husband you need to try and stay strong for not only your wife but also your kids. This is not something you can do alone, you need the guidance and direction from the Lord and you must take time to get alone and pray and ask God for help. It is not wrong to ask him why and express your feelings but know he is a loving God and He is the only one that can help you during this time. You may also need to find a man friend you can talk to outside of your family. This person should be a good friend and hopefully be someone that is spiritually grounded and is of strong faith. They must be someone you can trust and confide with and take time to fellowship together. Go have breakfast, golfing or fishing, just find the time to just meet and talk.

As the head of the house the man takes pride in being the provider but with a sickness of this magnitude, we need to now change our mindset. I researched and read what I could but it never prepared me for what I was going to encounter. There were people I ran into at work and in church that were facing the same situation and in two of the cases the husband refused to accept the cancer and they got bitter.

I found that when a man encounters this type of news it does one of two things. They accept it and try to do their best to adjust their life and it moves them closer to God. Then there are those that go into denial and blame God, which drives them away from the one source they need. They go into denial and with this attitude it creates a non-supporting role and causes more tension on the whole family.

I am not saying you need to be super spiritual and that you will be perfect in handling everything that comes your way. Just do your best and be supportive and encourage her. There will be times she will say things that she does not mean but learn to just listen and not try to correct her or give advice. This is something I still have a hard time trying to do to this day. Just be there and listen to her. Hear what her needs and wants are and ask how you can help. Do not force your agenda on her, let time take its course. She is processing and dealing with heavy stuff, so don't try to understand everything. We would not know until we were walking in her shoes. Show patience, humility, compassion and Love.

The most important thing you can do is to continue to lift her up in Prayer and be a positive conduit, feeding your surroundings with words of encouragement. Find the best out of your situation and meditate on those things. Believe that God will move in your situation and you "Will Conquer Cancer."

A Daughter as a Caregiver

The timing of my mom's diagnosis came at a good time. I had just became a Registered Nurse (RN) and I was still living at home. When my mom needed the Neupogen shots, I was able to give her those at home. That way she could go straight to work and not stop at the clinic for the shot.

I shaved my mom's head. She asked me if that was hard. Well it wasn't hard because I didn't feel it was a loss. I felt it was a blessing. The chemo was working and doing what it was supposed to do. It was something that brought us closer, so it wasn't hard for me.

Sure, I cried initially when I found out she had cancer. My husband, (my boyfriend at the time), reminded me that I called him crying. It is a normal re-action to such a diagnosis.

However, I don't like to get emotional and I put up walls when it comes to that. That's how I do what I do every day. I watch people die every day. I code people and some live and some die. While my fellow nurses and I look like we might be joking in the break room, it is how we deal with so much loss.

When it comes to family, I put up walls to at-tempt to deal. It is not the right way of doing things but it is what I have to do to survive with what I deal with in real life.

Paige

A Daughter as a Caregiver

I was 17 years old when I found out that my mother had cancer. I remember my parents sat my sister and I down the day after Christmas to let us know that my mom was diagnosed with stage III breast cancer. I realized that Christmas may never be the same again. When my parents made the announcement, I felt like my life had changed in a split second, more drastical-ly than I could ever imagine and it really made me see how fragile life was. That night I really needed some-one to talk to about the news I had heard and I con-fided in one of my newer friends, Josh. He was the only one I told for a couple weeks.

January 2009 started my last semester of high school and I had more responsibilities than ever. On top of keeping up with five Advanced Placement (AP) classes and trying to keep my GPA high enough for colleges, I began to take over responsibilities to keep up with household work and make dinner every night. I was glad to help but with all these responsibilities, I decided not to play softball my senior year of high school. It may not seem like a big deal to you but I had played softball since I was five years old and I was hoping to play softball in college. I don't regret not playing, I had more important things to take care of and knew if I played, I wouldn't have time to help out like I needed to. God had a bigger plan for my family and me, so even though I missed playing softball, I know I had so much more to look forward to.

A month into my semester, my AP English teacher noticed I wasn't acting like myself and my attention to the class had changed. She called me up to talk to her and when she asked if anything was going on at home, I told her my mom had cancer. She was very helpful through the semester and gave me extra help after school so that I could do well on my AP test. She also had students stay after school to walk the track with her, due to some health problems. Being able to get away from home twice a week after school and hang out with classmates and my teacher really helped me cope with my mother's health problem.

I graduated from high school and went to The University of Florida in the fall. It was harder to help out since I was two hours away and I felt very helpless but I tried my best to come home as often as my class schedule would allow me to. I'm happy to say my mother has been cancer free for six years and I thank God every day that he healed her.

Kelsey

A Mother as a Caregiver

Laura and Doug came to my home to tell me Laura had been diagnosed with breast cancer.

If I remember correctly, I asked what the doctors do next. Laura told me the steps leading up to surgery. Our family had been through many disappointments in this life prior to this situation and the Lord has been with us and kept us strong. We know His Word is for today, tomorrow and always. Whatever our problem, our Lord will give us strength to endure.

I had no doubt that Laura would survive all that she was about to go through. She had made goals for her future and with a spirit of determination; I knew she would complete her goals. My prayer was that every cancer cell in her body would be destroyed and she would be completely **Healed**.

Meme (Laura's mom)

A Mother-in-Law as a Caregiver

My name is Sharon Harmon. I am Laura's mother-in-law.

I was living in Albuquerque, New Mexico when I received a call from my son in Florida telling me about Laura's condition. She wanted to know if I would come and help out for a while. Of course, my answer was yes and I would stay as long as they needed me.

With a heavy and hurting heart, I flew down to help in whatever way I could. At a time like this, the whole family is in turmoil. No one knowing what was ahead but everyone praying for God's guidance and a healing touch for Laura.

I was to keep things around the house, take Laura for her chemo treatments and just be there whenever needed. My two granddaughters were so worried about their mother and now Nana was living there, also. It was an adjustment for all but we had God's grace and we knew that he was in control.

I remember the first time I took her for her treatment. We walked into this big room and it was lined with chairs where people sat to get these treatments. I was in awe at how many there were. All of this was a real wake up call for me. It's different when you see all this instead of just hearing about it. While they were getting her set up, I would go get her a cheese-burger, fries and drink. This was something she enjoyed and a tiny bit of enjoyment for her was a blessing. We would sit there and chat, which I enjoyed and she always worked on her journal and I would chat with others in there. Such very sad stories.

I wish I could have taken her place and spared her all the hurt she had to go through. A mother hurts when her child hurts. In my heart and mind, Laura is my daughter and I love her as such. Never having a daughter, I believed God gave me them when my sons married. Never take for granted what God blesses you with.

This whole cancer ordeal was not easy to go through. There were so many problems, setbacks and terrifying moments for her. But I am so proud of the attitude and determination she kept through it all. She will be a help and blessing to others.

Laura was blessed with help, love and prayers from her husband, who had the faith of Job, daughters, mother, family, friends, me and the precious love of Jesus who answers prayers.

Nanny (Doug's mom)

Cancer has the ability to interrupt so many lives. Don't let it. Cancer does not have to control your life. The power in living comes when you keep your schedule and routine the same.

Don't give away your power!

LIFE AFTER TREATMENT

L ife after treatment is all about being a **survivor**. Just recently, I was able to embrace being a survivor. I guess it was easy to pretend things didn't happen, but I'm reminded every day when I look in the mirror. I have 11 physical scars that I have learned to embrace. My scars do not define me but I have used them to **refine** me. Almost every day I am asked," How did you do it?" The honest answer to that is…I have a strong faith in God and

I refused to become a victim. Does that mean I was never sad or never had a bad day? Oh no! I had my moments but then I focused my attention on the fact that I was still standing. My girls were at pivotal transitions in their lives and I was at an important place in my career. I had goals to attain and I certainly wasn't going to let cancer keep me from achieving my goals.

Even today, there are difficult moments. I am particularly uneasy during the week before my mammogram and even while I'm sitting in the Women's Center. I'm fidgety like a racehorse about to be put in the starting gate. There are so many memories associated with the Women's Center, the surgical center, the hospital and the chemo lab.

Since my initial treatment, I've had a couple of biopsies that thankfully have been benign. I had a tricky lymph node in the left axilla, which was not the original area that kept lighting up on the PET Scan. So, I had a partial lymph node dissection on the left axilla as a precaution.

The most important message I want to tell you is that life is a gift. Am I breathing? Yes! Then, **I have a purpose and responsibility to go on**. Life goes on! I have a responsibility to live every day with a smile on my face because I am a survivor. Generations before me went through clinical trials so that I could benefit from Red Devil Chemo, Taxol, Herceptin, Arimidex and Femara.

Life goes on and I choose to be happy and ...LIVE!

WHERE ARE WE NOW?

Doug and I will be married 34 years in November of 2015. I am blessed to have a husband who really stayed with me through sickness and health. So many marriages suffer at the hands of cancer. I resigned my position as principal to become a full time Meme (grandma) and I love spending time with my grandchildren. I started a Facebook page https://www.facebook.com/laurasjourneyofhope and blog www.laurasjourneyofhope.com and now, I'm sharing my story and spreading the message of **hope and encouragement**. I enjoy traveling with Doug and spending time with family and friends.

I completed my first 5K walk for breast cancer. I did not realize that the survivors wore a different color shirt at the 5K run. It was a very emotional day. Complete strangers were cheering us on as we walked and after we crossed the finish line. It was truly and amazing experience. I walked for all who are **fighting** breast cancer. I walked to celebrate all **survivors** and to remember those who **lost their battle** to this horrible disease.

Below is a picture on my survivor shirt and medal. I walked in celebration of Cheryll and in memory of Nancy.

Kelsey is married to Josh. Yes, the same young man she confided in when she first found out about my diagnosis. They started dating, fell in love and eventually married in 2012. It was a busy year. She graduated from the University of Florida and was married 14 days later. She was a beautiful bride and is employed in the medical field.

Paige married Case in January 2010 and they now have three children. Paige jokes that she has been in school since she started kindergarten and in a way, give or take a semester, it's true. Paige is a working mommy and continues her education, aspiring to become a Nurse Practioner.

Take pride in how far you've come
and have faith in how far you can go.
In all of life's craziness, remember to enjoy the
journey.

Laura Starner, B.S., M.S., is an author, wife, mother, grandmother, retired school principal and an encourager at heart.

After 23 years in education, Laura retired her position as a school administrator. She brings that experience to lead and inspire others to live a life full of hope and to reach their full potential. Through her blog she encourages survivors, caregivers, friends and family to live each day to the fullest.

Laura Starner holds a B.S. in Elementary Education and a M.S. in Educational Leadership. She has been happily married for 33 years and has two children and three grandchildren.

Laura exudes positivity and naturally encourages those around her. She believes that everyone can live a powerful life. She enjoys eating clean and trying new recipes. She loves to read, especially at the beach, and telling her story through her blog. Most importantly, she loves and adores her ever-expanding family!

APPENDIX A - TIMELINE

2008

December 3 – Primary Care Physician

December 17 – Mammogram

December 19 – Biopsy

December 26 - On call physician told me I had breast cancer (over the phone)

December 29- Appointment with Surgical Oncologist who told me how *LUCKY* I was to have breast cancer

December 31 – Appointment with Hematologist – Oncologist who would soon be known as Dr. Wonderful

2009

January 5 – Bone Scan

January 6 – Chemo Education and remove acrylic nails

January 7 – PET Scan

January 8 – MUGA Scan

January 12 – 1st PORT Surgery

January 14 – Breast MRI

January 15 – 1st Red Devil Chemo

January 29 – 2nd Red Devil Chemo

January 31 – Shaved Head

February 11 – Breast Surgeon (Second opinion…leaving the doctor who thought I was lucky to have breast cancer)

February 12 – 3rd Red Devil Chemo

February 17 – PICC Line inserted because PORT looked suspicious on February 12th

February 26- 4th and LAST Red Devil Chemo

March 1 – Low grade fever started

March 9 – March 16th - Hospitalized with fever. Received intravenous antibiotics.

March 10 – PORT removed. Must use the PICC line for chemo.

March 23 – Taxol and Herceptin

March 30 – Herceptin

March 31 – Appointment with Plastic Surgeon who would operate simultaneously with the Breast Surgeon.

April 7 – Taxol and Herceptin Kelsey's Awards Ceremony at school

April 14 – Herceptin

April 21– Taxol and Herceptin

April 28 – Herceptin

May 5 – Taxol and Herceptin (Last one)

May 12 – Herceptin

May 19 – Herceptin

May 26 – Herceptin and Kelsey's Baccalaureate

May 27 –Cheri arrived from New Mexico

May 28 – Senior Awards – May 29th – Graduation

May 31 – Kelsey's Graduation Party

June 3 – Major Surgery

June 16 – Second Surgery – Margin revision

June 24 – Dr. Wonderful

June 25 – Plastic Surgeon follow up

July 2 – Breast Surgeon – Surgical Drains removed

July 6 – ECHO

July 9 – Begin Herceptin again

July 20 – Radiation Simulation and Herceptin

July 21– Radiation walk through – set machines

July 22 – Radiation begins (35 rounds – go M-F for 35 days)

July 31 - Herceptin

August 3 – Back to work

September 10 – Last day of radiation!

2010

March (Mid) – last Herceptin!

Made in the USA
Coppell, TX
03 August 2021